MW00604212

Suddenly ALONE

Three steps for your financial clarity as a recent widow

SECOND EDITION

by Laura Amendola, CFP®
Founder

wealthcare4widows®

All of the profits and royalties received from the sale of this guidebook are donated for charitable purposes to provide scholarships, services, and emergency family support to widows in need.

Second Edition Copyright 2015© by Laura Amendola, CFP®
First Edition Copyright 1999© by Laura Amendola, CFP®

All rights reserved. Without limiting the rights under copyright reserved above, no part of this publication may be reproduced, stored in, or introduced into a retrieval system, or transmitted, in any form, or by any means (electronic, mechanical, photocopying, recording, or otherwise) without the prior written permission of both the copyright owner and the above publisher of this book.

Designed by Lisa Valuyskaya
Cover design by Lisa Valuyskaya
Printed in the United States of America
ISBN: 978-0-9972073-0-9

*To my beloved father
Frank Brown,
who taught me
the importance of
helping others.*

*You will forever be with
my mother and I in
thought and spirit.
We miss you.*

TABLE OF CONTENTS

Preface

When I was a little girl, I can remember several times I woke up in the middle of a cold night in Florida because the phone was ringing. We didn't have that many super cold nights, but boy, when we did, it was *cold*. I would hear my dad finally get to the phone and usually say something like, "I'll take care of it. I'll be right there."

This was back before old homes were re-done with central air and heat, so people stored heating oil in a tank outside their home. My dad would quickly get dressed, and then he would leave moments later. I remember now how the lights would fade away on my bedroom wall, since he parked his truck on that side of our home. My parents owned an oil distributorship, and he would go in the middle of the night, climb up on a platform to load a kerosene truck in the freezing cold weather, drive out into the country, and help an elderly widow (that's who had called) by refilling her heating tank.

It's what you did. You showed up for people. He never minded that call. He seemed honored to have received the call. We never had an unlisted number (I still don't and don't mind my clients knowing my home or cell number). My dad always showed up for anyone who called needing help.

However, life doesn't always go as planned. When I was only 17, my father died in a car accident. After his unexpected death, my mother faced tremendous challenges. This included selling the family business, dealing with the financial change, and being a widow at 53. Despite all the challenges, my mother helped me finish my four-year degree.

I have a firsthand appreciation for the difficulties widows face, having seen my mother go through it. She is my role model for being a strong, independent woman. Championing a widow with the belief that she is capable and strong is why I come to work every day. I find deep joy in the connections that happen when I work directly with my clients. I am proud to be a member of her team of professionals, and be that person she can rely on to get things done.

Now, when I reflect on my relationships with others, both personal and professional, I realize that I value showing up for people. It's in everything I do. In my practice, I deliver "heating oil" to widows so that they can get through those coldest nights.

Introduction

MOVING TOWARD CLARITY

There is a strong connection between understanding your finances and your emotional recovery. The depth of pain and shock experienced as a widow can cause immediate paralysis. You are suddenly alone, overwhelmed, and powerless to do anything more than ride along on a turbulent sea of sorrow and distress. The grief that follows a death is the most profound of all emotional experiences.

Grieving while facing a lack of financial information or stability can cause debilitating anxiety that would weaken anybody's emotional healing. I've seen a widow with an estate full of millions act "poor" long after probate and taxes have been finalized.

You Can Do It!

YOU ARE CAPABLE of handling your financial affairs. You do not have to be an expert. You just need to stay involved and find experts to help you. Rely on their expertise and clarity of thought. The death of a spouse is often the single most traumatic event any of my clients have had to experience. This book is a guide to help you move forward into your new financial future. Nothing works as well as a little knowledge and organization.

Simple addition and subtraction will tell you the two most important things you need to know: what you are worth, and how your expenses balance out against your income. Once done, you will better answer all those nagging questions such as, "Am I going to make it?" and "Do I have enough?", "Can I afford to keep my house or my car?", or "Do I need to go back to work?"

Decision Making While Grief Stricken

Grief causes confusion. The brain is functioning differently. There are several levels of conscious thinking going on at the same time. You are not going crazy. Most all widows seem to experience some memory loss and confusion during this period. Scientifically, it's called "cognitive disconnect." **This is why you must write everything down.**

The initial twelve months following your husband's death is what I call the "year of transition." It is important to realize that your judgment—your ability to make the right decisions— during this emotionally trying time may become impaired.

No Radical Actions

Often, there is a sense of deprivation, sadness, and disorientation, which makes you particularly vulnerable to the misuse of money. You need to understand what your resources are, where they are, and what they are doing to provide you with the new foundation you will use to rebuild your life. During the first year after your husband's death, keep a higher amount of savings than usual while your income and expenses are transitioning. You will need readily available cash, not only to support you during this period, but also to enable you to pay debts and funeral expenses. Over the next year, you will have time to assess your financial situation more thoroughly.

During this time, there are several pitfalls to avoid: take no drastic action such as selling your house, quitting your job, moving in with or closer to your family, buying insurance, lending or giving money to a family member/friend, or making any major investments.

This Guide

The Wealthcare4Widows® financial planning process involves three stages unique to a widow – Organize, Recover, and Renew. This eBook will present a review of the first stage: Getting Organized. There are three financial concepts within this stage vital to providing you more immediate stability as you begin your journey:

These concepts are presented in the order I have found most effective and productive for our clients. As you progress through the entire Wealthcare4Widows® process over time, it will help you plan for yourself and your family, and ultimately help bring you the clarity, confidence, and comfort you are seeking.

We've made this as easy and straightforward to read as possible. No legalese and all jargon defined. You can read this in sections, skip around the parts you need to know at the moment, or bring this in as a reference when working with your team of professionals.

Most of this can be done over the course of the first year. No rush. If you are worried you are missing something important, we have marked the **critical items to be done in the first 60 days** with the symbol 🦆 0-60 DAYS . You can do a quick scan through and make sure nothing critical has been missed.

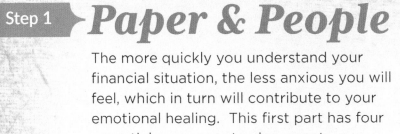

Step 1 ▶ Paper & People

The more quickly you understand your financial situation, the less anxious you will feel, which in turn will contribute to your emotional healing. This first part has four essential components: document gathering, list of bills, probate of the will, and settlement of the estate.

DOCUMENT GATHERING

To start, begin to make distinct piles on the dining room table or other designated area. You can make more elaborate filing systems later if you choose. For now, the basic system of labeling the stacks with sticky notes will work just fine.

Important Papers

- ☐ Death certificate
- ☐ Marriage license
- ☐ Birth certificates
- ☐ The original will
- ☐ Trust documents
- ☐ Insurance policies
- ☐ Account statements

- ☐ Social Security numbers
- ☐ Veteran's discharge papers
- ☐ Naturalization papers
- ☐ Business agreements (Buy/Sell)
- ☐ Property deeds
- ☐ Loan documents
- ☐ Tax returns (last two years)

Make a List of Important Bills

Open any mail piled up and make a list of important bills – mortgage payments, utilities, car payments, health and auto insurance. Share this list with the executor of the estate if it is not you.

Pay only essential bills in joint name or the bills that are due immediately so as not to incur late payment fees (omit your husband's major medical bills for now).

0-60 DAYS Be especially mindful of **auto and homeowner's insurance** because they do not provide grace periods and can cancel your policies for non-payment.

CONTACT YOUR ATTORNEY & FILE FOR PROBATE OF THE WILL

It has been observed that widows who seek professional help with various aspects of their emotional and financial situations progress more quickly to a state of well-being than those who try to do it all themselves. At this stage, it will most likely be easiest to work with an attorney whom your husband has already dealt with. Settling an estate is not an easy task, nor is finding a new attorney while you are grieving.

0-60 DAYS Should you find that your husband died intestate (without a will), you now face estate planning's worst scenario. The state will have complete power to determine the disposition of your husband's estate. **Contact an attorney immediately.**

Determine who the executor of the will is and who the trustee is of any trust that exists. Usually this will be you, the surviving spouse. If you are able to locate your husband's will and other legal documents easily, sit down and review them. Place a call to your attorney to verify any questions you have and to inquire if you need to file for a new tax identification number for your husband's estate. You will need to obtain this number to open an account at your bank in the name of his estate, if necessary.

A Power of Attorney document for your husband is no longer valid due to his death. You may no longer use this document to transact business for him or sign his name.

Begin the Estate Settlement Process

In the majority of cases, the surviving spouse becomes responsible for the administration of the deceased spouse's estate. Thus, you become the "Personal Representative" or "Executrix" of your husband's estate.

0-60 DAYS If you are not acting in this capacity, you may want to **hire an attorney to represent your interests as an heir or beneficiary.**

You may also become the "Successor Trustee" of any trusts in existence or being created during settlement. The courts require that you perform many legal responsibilities regarding probate.

What Exactly is Probate?

Probate is a court-supervised process for identifying and gathering the assets of a deceased person (decedent), paying the decedent's debts, and distributing the decedent's assets to his or her beneficiaries.

Not all property will have to pass through the probate process. You must sort out all the assets your husband owned or partially owned by your husband and file an inventory with the probate court within 90 days of his death. Property ownership gets more complicated if the complexities of common law versus community property statutes must be applied.

Transferring of Assets

The probate process proves that the will of a deceased person is valid so their property can, in due course, be retitled or transferred to beneficiaries of the will.

0-60 DAYS In some states, you must file a will **within a certain number of days after death.**

The probate court will issue letters of appointment certifying the authority of the personal representative to handle the estate. You will be required to supply these letters in order to transfer assets at banks, investment firms, and other entities.

Get Assistance

Obviously, this is not going to be an easy task, and I strongly urge you to delegate this responsibility to a legal professional. Most likely, you are not in the best emotional condition to take on a project of this magnitude, which will require a lot of detail work and learning new facts.

> **A well-equipped law firm will be able to take care of locating and collecting assets far faster than you would by yourself, in most cases.**

Due to their experience, they are able to review bank records and tax returns quickly to discover assets you might not be aware of. They will also have contact information for insurance companies and other entities to expedite claim for assets.

0-60 DAYS If your husband was involved in any kind of litigation prior to death, had significant debts, was killed in an accident, owned a business or a partial interest in a business, owned real estate in another state, or was having a controversy with any taxing authority, **you definitely need legal assistance.**

Estate Tax Return

Your attorney will determine whether or not a federal (and one or more state) estate tax returns are necessary for your husband's estate. If you are the personal representative of the estate, you are personally liable to the IRS for preparing these returns within nine months, which are quite different from the income tax returns most people are familiar with. The estate attorney and tax preparer will work together to help you.

Step 2 **_Stabilizing Your Cash Flow_**

Step Two of your new financial future is about accessing all the benefits available to you, clarifying your income and expenses, and updating all your insurance policies.

APPLY FOR BENEFITS

As a surviving spouse, you may be eligible for various benefits. You will need to file claims for each asset. The most common are social security, veteran, and pension benefits. Current or former employers provide some benefits. The human resources department will help you through this process. Remember to inquire about all employee benefits, including accrued vacation pay, final wages, or commissions earned (but not yet paid), as well as pending medical reimbursements.

Make a Document Travel Bag:

Keep these documents with you as you visit the various offices to apply for benefits: death certificates, birth certificates (all family members), social security numbers, marriage license, military discharge papers, and bank account numbers.

Social Security Benefits

You earn entitlement to social security benefits through work credits and payment of social security taxes. This federal program provides benefits to many – but not all – surviving spouses and some dependent children under several different programs. You can be eligible for spousal benefits even if you have never contributed to social security. If you are caring for at least one child of the decedent who is eligible for child's benefits and is age 16 or younger or who is disabled, you are also eligible for benefits. Child's benefits are for unmarried children under 18 (or up to 19 if they are attending elementary or secondary school). There is also a one-time, lump-sum death benefit of $255 available if eligible.

To apply for benefits, you will need:

- ☐ State certified death certificate for your spouse.
- ☐ Your husband's social security number.
- ☐ Your own social security number.
- ☐ A state certified copy of your own birth certificate.
- ☐ A state certified copy of your marriage certificate.
- ☐ Any dependent children's social security numbers.
- ☐ Your husband's most recent W-2 form or any federal self-employment tax return (these will usually be attached to the most recent income tax return he filed).
- ☐ Name and account number of a bank account where you want your benefits to be direct deposited.

Because of the complexities, this information is not intended to be a complete summary of social security. It is meant to serve as merely a guide to get you started, covering only the most common situations. Call to make an appointment with your local social security office to discuss what benefits may be available for you. To learn more, see my detailed article *Social Security Survivor's Benefits: How Much Can A Widow Receive & When?*

Veterans Benefits

If your husband was given an honorable discharge, you may be eligible to payments for burial expenses as well as other benefits, including survivors' pension, educational benefits for children, and medical care for some spouses and children. Many veterans also maintained service-related life insurance. To get information and make claims, you will need an official copy of your spouse's Veteran's DD-214, which is the official discharge form for military service. If you cannot find this document for your spouse, you can request one from the National Personnel Records Center by submitting the appropriate request form.

www.archives.gov/veterans/military-service-records

Department of Veterans Affairs
www.va.gov or call 800.827.1000

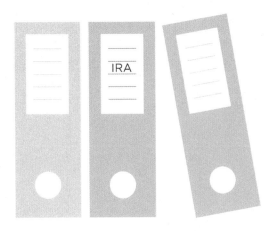

Pension & Retirement Benefits

Pension plans are also known as defined benefit plans. If your husband was receiving pension income, notify the pension plan administrator of the death and inquire as to what benefits are available to you as a surviving spouse. If he was still working at the time of his death, be sure to ask his employer's human resources department if there are pension benefits you qualify for now or in the future.

Because it is so common now for people to change jobs frequently during their careers, you should also contact all of his former employers to make the same inquiry.

Unions administer pension plans, so if your husband was a union member, contact that union for pension benefit information.

Most employer sponsored retirement plans are known as defined contribution plans. The two most common are 401(k) plans and profit sharing plans. The retirement plan documents will explain what distribution options are available to you. In most cases, the surviving spouse will have the right to transfer the plan account balance into an IRA (Individual Retirement Account) at any financial institution the spouse chooses.

The transfer must be directly from the retirement plan sponsor to the new IRA custodian. If you take possession of the plan assets, you will have to pay income taxes on all taxable portions of the funds you receive.

Several types of IRAs will provide you different options as a surviving spouse regarding future withdrawal capabilities. **Please note:** If your husband is holding any company stock within a retirement plan, you will want to speak with your financial planner or accountant regarding advanced planning that you should do pertaining to the transfer of any company stock to an IRA **before the transfer.**

The rules governing retirement plan and IRA assets are complex. The penalty for making mistakes as well as missed tax opportunities with regard to company stock can be significant. Get the advice you need to be sure you understand what you are doing with these assets and that you have complete information on the options available for your specific situation.

Life Insurance Benefits

Notify the insurance agent or company to file the necessary claims. If you are not sure if your husband carried life insurance on himself, go online or to the checkbook and review an entire year's entries to see if there are any premium payments listed. Often, policies are kept in a bank safe deposit box – another place to look. In addition to personally owned life insurance, also check with his employer since life insurance coverage can be provided under a group policy at his work.

After determining your husband's death benefits payable, if there are any beneficiaries other than yourself, you will need to advise them on the distribution of the proceeds. Beneficiaries of life insurance do not pay income tax on the proceeds received.

> **There are many options as what to do with life insurance proceeds. Many widows assume they should immediately pay off an existing mortgage. This is not always the best utilization of the proceeds.**

First, you should carefully consider the use of a large amount of cash as part of a comprehensive financial plan. Larger estates may even have the spouse 'disclaim' some or all of the insurance in favor of the children as a method of post-mortem estate tax planning. Hence, be sure to collaborate with your estate attorney and accountant **before making the claim.**

If you are the beneficiary of the proceeds, you may have various payment options of how to receive the money. Carefully evaluate the options, as these proceeds will become part of the bigger picture of your overall financial situation. Many times, it is important to keep money liquid during the estate settlement period, as assets are often frozen during the probate process. Social security benefits, as well as retirement benefits, may take a while to receive.

While you are managing your grief, consider putting all life insurance proceeds into cash alternative securities, savings accounts, or short term certificates of deposits maturing in less than one year. Give yourself time to heal before evaluating any new financial decisions regarding this money.

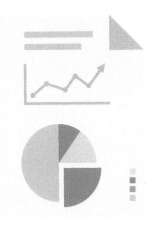

Annuity Benefits

These policies are investments made with insurance companies and are acquired from insurance agents, financial professionals, and even banks. If your husband owned an annuity and he named you the beneficiary, you may be able to create (or continue) a regular stream of income for yourself. Older policies will often have higher payout amounts compared to what is available today.

An annuity policy looks very much the same as a life insurance binder and can usually be found in a file or safe deposit box. Account statements are typically generated annually or quarterly. The first step is to call the annuity company and notify them of your husband's passing. This doesn't have to be done immediately and can wait until you feel more capable making decisions. **Before taking any action with your annuity, ask these three questions:** Do I need this income? What payout options are available to me? How will taking a lump-sum affect my taxes? Carefully consider the many payment options available with your professional advisors before surrendering an annuity.

Property Tax Exemption Benefit

This exemption varies by state with regard to amount and eligibility. Call or visit your local agency that collects your property tax so they can tell you exactly what exemptions are offered to you as a widow. Often the true benefit comes from making sure existing exemptions, already in place prior to your husband's passing, such as disability, military service, age, etc., will be continued.

Financial Aid Benefits

This benefit is often overlooked. Be sure to contact the financial aid office if you have a child in college. Your son or daughter may be eligible for special assistance or increased financial aid. Counselors are more than happy to assist you to help determine any possible increased eligibility. If your son or daughter is over the age 18, they will most likely need to be on the phone when you call the Financial Aid Office, due to new privacy communication restrictions.

EVALUATE YOUR INCOME AND EXPENSES

Completing the income and expense worksheet is the single most important task to help reduce your stress and worry as a widow. Simple addition and subtraction is all you need to begin moving forward with clarity about your finances.

In general, you want an idea of what it takes to maintain your standard of living with as few disruptions as possible. You may discover you need more income than you are currently receiving. **Do not panic if this happens to you.** Your financial professionals can help you rectify the situation. In the next chapter you will review your assets and liabilities to determine if any should be repositioned to provide you with the additional income you need.

Using the information about what benefits are available for you, let's begin to estimate what income you can expect to receive. Under the income category, list everything you are sure you will receive. The first page of your tax return can be very helpful to determine what income amounts have been coming in prior to the death of your husband and from what source. If you work, include your employment income. Check for income from promissory notes, rental properties, or a business interest. You are likely to continue receiving the income from these items if you inherit the assets.

Next, find out how you spend your income. Review your checkbook or the online transaction history of your bank accounts to determine what your expenses have been. Begin to enter your fixed living expenses into the worksheet - housing, transportation, food, and healthcare are the big items to fill in first.

By going back through last year's history of expenses, items often overlooked will emerge, such as gifts, clothing, and travel. These are called discretionary expenses, and are important to know in order to project what you are accustomed to spending.

Now that you have calculated your income and expenses, total both categories to find out if you have more than enough income (positive cash flow) or insufficient income (negative cash flow). **Remember you are still in the fact-gathering stage, so don't panic if you have a negative cash flow.** Consult with your financial professionals to help you rectify the situation. Conversely, you may find you have sufficient income to cover your current expenses. Resist any spree-spending at this stage. Keep your long-term situation in mind. What is sufficient income today may not be ten years from now. When planning, work with your advisors to plan for changing expenses and to help your income keep pace with inflation.

From here, you can find solutions that will be important to maintain a healthy mental attitude regarding your money as you move forward on your own.

INCOME AND EXPENSE WORKSHEET

	MONTHLY	ANNUALLY
SOURCES OF INCOME		
Salary & Earned Income	$	$
Pension	$	$
Social Security	$	$
Rental Income	$	$
Dividends, Interest, CapGain	$	$
Other:	$	$
TOTAL INCOME		$
LIABILITIES		
Mortgage Payment or Rent	$	$
Home Equity Loan Payment	$	$
Automobile Loans(s)	$	$
Credit Card Payments	$	$
Other:	$	$
TOTAL LIABILITIES		$
TAXES		
Federal Income Taxes	$	$
State & Intangible Taxes	$	$
Local & Other Property Taxes	$	$
FICA & Medicare Withholding	$	$
Other:	$	$
TOTAL TAXES		$

	MONTHLY	ANNUALLY

INSURANCE

	MONTHLY	ANNUALLY
Life (premium payments)	$	$
Health & Dental	$	$
Disability	$	$
Auto	$	$
Homeowners	$	$
Other:	$	$
TOTAL INSURANCE		$

TRANSPORTATION

	MONTHLY	ANNUALLY
Gas	$	$
Maintenance & Repair	$	$
License, Registration	$	$
Public Transportation	$	$
Other:	$	$
TOTAL TRANSPORTATION		$

CONTRIBUTIONS

	MONTHLY	ANNUALLY
Religious	$	$
Charitable	$	$
TOTAL CONTRIBUTIONS		$

	MONTHLY	ANNUALLY

HOUSEHOLD EXPENSES

	MONTHLY	ANNUALLY
Groceries	$	$
Clothing	$	$
Doctor & Dentist	$	$
Prescription Drugs	$	$
Personal Care	$	$
Electricity/Gas	$	$
Phone/Internet	$	$
Cable/Satellite	$	$
Water/Water Conditioners	$	$
Garbage	$	$
Pest Control	$	$
Home Maintenance & Repair	$	$
Pool Maintenance & Repair	$	$
Security Systems	$	$
Home Furnishings	$	$
Dining Out	$	$
Recreation, Entertain, Hobbies	$	$
Education Expenses	$	$
Daycare	$	$
Veterinarian & Pet Care	$	$
Book, Magazines, Other	$	$
Club or Membership Dues	$	$
Vacation & Travel	$	$
Gifts	$	$
Professional Fees	$	$
Others:	$	$

TOTAL HOUSEHOLD EXPENSES $

ANNUAL SUMMARY TOTAL INCOME $

ANNUAL SUMMARY TOTAL EXPENSES (-) $

DISCRETIONARY INCOME = $

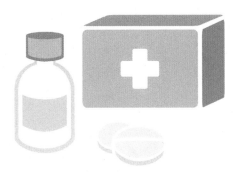

Health Insurance

Health insurance is the one major exception to the rule in that you don't need to make any financial decisions in a hurry. It is important to continue paying premiums, understand and evaluate your coverage, and complete any necessary forms to continue coverage if you are widowed under age 65.

If your husband had your health insurance through his employer, you are eligible for continued coverage for thirty-six months. However, you should expect to pay a different amount for coverage, often a significantly higher amount, than your husband did. You will not have to show evidence of insurability to continue coverage.

0-60 DAYS There is typically a sixty-day deadline to file forms to secure continued benefits.

For cost comparison, another source for health insurance is individual private coverage available directly through a health insurance company or insurance representative. When evaluating health insurance policies, the premium cost is obviously the first consideration. It is very important to get clear information about deductibles, co-payment amounts, the availability of doctors and hospitals provided for coverage by each plan, as well as prescription coverage. If you need help, review all options with your financial planner to determine which may be best for you.

If your husband was in the military, TRICARE is a health care program for active duty service members, National Guard and Reserve members, retirees, their families, survivors, certain former spouses, and others registered in the Defense Enrollment Eligibility Reporting System (DEERS). Visit www.tricare.mil to obtain eligibility requirements.

Perhaps your husband was already retired. If this is the case, health insurance may have been provided as a retirement benefit. Check to see if there will be any changes to your current benefits. If you are over 65, you may already be enrolled in Medicare as well as supplemental policies. It will be important for you to understand what your current coverage is and continue to pay the premiums. Aim to have at least general knowledge of your Medicare benefits if you do not already know them. You can find Medicare information at www.medicare.gov.

Auto, Property, & Liability Insurance

Adjusting property, liability, and auto insurance is the most common task overlooked by surviving spouses.

After you notify the insurance companies, they will remove your husband as an insured on the policies. You most likely need the same dollar amounts you already have in place for coverage on your properties. However, if you received a large amount of life insurance proceeds, you may now need to increase your liability coverage. Review this coverage carefully to be sure the amount is enough to cover all of your property values and financial assets.

Connecting Your Financial Snapshots

Identifying assets and debts in an organized manner to get a snapshot of your current financial picture is Step Three of your new financial future.

It is likely, you will be making decisions about large sums of money – or what at first might seem like large sums of money. You may have received cash from life insurance or the assets of a retirement plan or IRA. There is no hurry to "figure out what to do." You have time. It is okay to allow a year to pass before you begin financial planning about your future needs and goals.

Resist any advice to put your money in longer-term investments at this time. Remember, your goal right now is only to gather information about the assets available to you. Don't make any long-term commitments until later, when you have completed a comprehensive financial plan.

NET WORTH WORKSHEET

When you calculated your income and expenses, you might have discovered that there did not seem to be enough income to cover your expenses. The next step is to determine what assets you have that may provide you with other sources of income besides social security and pension income. To do this, figure out your personal net worth. Calculating your net worth is simply listing what you own and then subtracting from that number the amount you owe (omit major medical bills for now).

Assets are defined as anything *you own* that has an exchange value if you sell it. *Personal Property* includes your home, vacations homes (or timeshares), cars, boats, home furnishings, and other items such as: jewelry, antiques, Oriental rugs, or art. *Personal Investments* are considered items such as cash, bank and/or investment accounts, stocks, stock-options, bonds, notes receivables, deferred annuities, retirement accounts, and investment real estate such as rental properties.

Liabilities are defined as any debts *you owe* to anyone. Once you have a list of your assets and their approximate value, you can begin listing the money you owe other people. The most common are home mortgages, auto loans, and credit cards.

While you are gathering information on outstanding loans, request the following: balance amount owed, maturity date, current payment, and current interest rate. This information will be helpful later when doing more comprehensive planning.

Should you discover any *contingent liabilities*, which is the potential obligation to pay a debt, let your professional advisors know this when you discover it. An example would be your husband may have personally guaranteed a loan your son or daughter took out to start a business or buy a piece of equipment. If they fail to make payments, your husband's estate may be liable. Another common contingent liability is a signed pledge to a charity that is not mentioned in his will. The charity may or may not be entitled to be paid. Your attorney can help you with this one.

Property Titles & Beneficiary Designations

Your net worth worksheet will also help you to identify investments, vehicles, and properties to be re-titled later such as your homes, autos, bank accounts, or safe deposit box.

In addition, you may discover accounts with beneficiary designations also needing to be updated.

When you are ready, you can talk with your bank, attorney, and financial planner to help you with these tasks. For now, I suggest circling assets on the worksheet which may need to be re-titled and placing a square around the assets to check on later that might need a beneficiary update.

Joint Checking Account

It is a good idea to keep your checking account in joint name open for a year or so.

Checks may still come payable to your husband for some time. You'll be able to deposit these checks into your joint account. Avoid the common mistake of adding children to your accounts. There are legal ramifications that can cause many problems in the future by doing this.

Business Ownership

Perhaps the most challenging situation you will face as a widow is if your husband was the owner or partner of a business. Valuing a business can be complex after the death of it's owner. Unfortunately, what to do with the business is a daunting task that must be addressed during your time of grief. Depending on your own involvement in the operations, the essential question usually is, "Should I maintain, sell, or close the business?" Each decision can have very different monetary outcomes.

To help you make smart decisions, work closely with your financial planner, attorney and accountant. They can assist you with determining the current value of the business and what income you can expect to receive from it. In some cases, there may already be an agreement in place with other owners or a competitor to buy the business from you. Usually, if this buy-sell agreement exists, they will contact you quickly in order to continue the day-to-day activities of the business. To learn more see my detailed article *Business Ownership as a Part of Your Husband's Estate*.

NET WORTH WORKSHEET

ASSETS	CURRENT VALUE

CASH & CASH EQUIVALENTS

Checking accounts	$
Savings accounts	$
Money market accounts	$
Savings bonds	$
CD's (certificates of deposit)	$
Cash value of life insurance (yours)	$
Expected value of life insurance proceeds (if not listed in savings already above)	$
TOTAL CASH	$

INVESTED ASSETS

Taxable accounts

Brokerage	$
Other:	$

Retirement accounts

IRA	$
Roth IRA	$
401(k) or 403(b)	$
SEP-IRA or SIMPLE IRA	$
Keogh or other qualified plan	$
Pension (vested benefit)	$
Annuity (accumulated value)	$

Business ownership interests

Real estate (rental property or land)	$
Business entities	$
TOTAL INVESTED ASSETS	$

ASSETS	CURRENT VALUE

PERSONAL USE ASSETS

Principal home	$
Vacation home	$
Autos, RV's, boats	$
Home furnishings	$
Art, antiques, coins, collectibles	$
Jewelry, furs	$
Other:	$
TOTAL USE ASSETS	$
TOTAL ASSETS (CASH + INVESTED ASSETS + USE ASSETS)	$

LIABILITIES	BALANCE OWED

CURRENT

Credit cards	$
Estimated income tax owed	$
Other outstanding bills	$

LONG-TERM

Home mortgage	$
Home equity loan	$
Mortgages on rental properties	$
Auto loans	$
Student loans	$
Life insurance policy loans	$
Other long-term debt	$
TOTAL LIABILITIES	$
NET WORTH (TOTAL ASSETS - TOTAL LIABILITIES)	$

IN SUMMARY

The Wealthcare4Widows® financial planning process is about gaining clarity. There are three stages unique to a widow – Organize, Recover, and Renew.

> **The more quickly you understand your financial situation, the less anxious you will feel, which in turn contributes to your emotional healing.**

This guide presented a review of the first stage: Getting Organized. The process of Getting Organized has three steps:

In **Step One** you sort through papers and people. Collect all your documents. Create a list of your important bills. Contact your attorney to file for probate of the will. Begin the estate settlement process.

In **Step Two** you stabilize your new cash flow. Apply for the benefits you are eligible for. Evaluate your income and expenses. Adjust your insurance coverages.

In **Step Three** you connect your financial snapshots. Complete your net worth worksheet to organize your assets and liabilities. Determine if any assets should be repositioned to provide you with additional income. Identify properties needing to be re-titled or a change of beneficiary in the future. Keep your joint checking account open to deposit any checks you might receive payable to your husband. Work closely with your financial professionals if your husband owned a business.

YOU ARE CAPABLE of handling your financial affairs. Maintain a willingness to learn and couple it with asking for sound financial advice. Don't take any radical actions. As you are ready, work with your team of professionals and start to step into your financial future. Over time, I am confident your knowledge will evolve into vision and strength.

Next up are the stages of Recover and Renew. Recover is about opening up life through conversations that allow you to have a deeper awareness of your values. These conversations create a curiosity for all that is possible, which often includes a personal resourcefulness to evolve, grow, and expand from the loss of your husband. Renew is about addressing your financial situation and being ready to take a comprehensive look at other issues that affect your life both now and in the future. Look for more books on these topics.

For more information about the Wealthcare4Widows® process as well as additional resources and tools, please visit www.Wealthcare4Widows.com

Don't hesitate to contact me. You can reach me directly at Laura@Wealthcare4Widows.com

The information contained in this book does not purport to be a complete description of the securities, markets, or developments referred to in this material. The information has been obtained from sources considered to be reliable, but we do not guarantee that the foregoing material is accurate or complete. Any information is not a complete summary or statement of all available data necessary for making an investment decision and does not constitute a recommendation. Any opinions of the chapter authors are those of the chapter author and not necessarily those of RJFS or Raymond James. Expressions of opinion are as of the initial book publishing date and are subject to change without notice. Raymond James Financial Services, Inc. is not responsible for the consequences of any particular transaction or investment decision based on the content of this book. All financial, retirement and estate planning should be individualized as each person's situation is unique. This information is not intended as a solicitation or an offer to buy or sell any security referred to herein. Keep in mind that there is no assurance that our recommendations or strategies will ultimately be successful or profitable nor protect against a loss. There may also be the potential for missed growth opportunities that may occur after the sale of an investment. Recommendations, specific investments or strategies discussed may not be suitable for all investors. Past performance may not be indicative of future results. You should discuss any tax or legal matters with the appropriate professional.

Made in the USA
Columbia, SC
11 March 2022

57552039R00024